My Mind Is Out to Get Me

My Mind Is Out to Get Me

Humor and Wisdom in Recovery

compiled and written by
Dr. Ron B.

HAZELDEN®

Hazelden Educational Materials
Center City, Minnesota 55012-0176

Library of Congress Cataloging in Publication Data
My mind is out to get me : humor and wisdom in recovery / compiled and written by Dr. Ron B.
   p. cm.
Collection of slogans and sayings compiled from participants at Alcoholics Anonymous
meetings.
   ISBN: 1-56838-010-0
   1. Alcoholics Anonymous—Humor. 2. Alcoholics Anonymous—Quotations, maxims, etc.
3. Alcoholism—Psychological aspects—Quotations, maxims, etc. I. B., Ron.
PN6231.A448M9 1994
818'.540208—dc20   93-42421
                                                 CIP

Editor's note

    Hazelden Educational Materials offers a variety of information on chemical dependency
and related areas. Our publications do not necessarily represent Hazelden's programs, nor do
they officially speak for any Twelve Step organization.

Preface

The highway ends at Galveston Island, Texas, USA. That's where my drinking ended also. On a January night in 1988, I held an almost-empty bottle of whiskey in one hand and a fully loaded .38 in the other. I didn't know which to put to my mouth next. For reasons I still don't fully understand, I put them both down. Through the grace of my Higher Power, and the program and fellowship of Alcoholics Anonymous, I have not needed to pick up either again.

Early in my recovery, I attended a meeting where the chairperson asked us to share our favorite slogan. I didn't know what she was talking about. Thankfully, others did. I was amazed at what I heard and eagerly inquired where these sayings were published so that I might obtain a copy. As far as I could determine, they were then and still are today, for the most part, unrecorded.

So I began carrying a notebook with me to write down these small bits of wisdom as they were shared in meetings. Many that appear here are reported exactly as they were spoken. Others were suggested by a member's shared experience, strength, and hope; I simply added the words.

I found that I listened better in meetings. And that one meeting at a time, the rich oral tradition of AA sayings and slogans was revealed. These sayings capture the spiritual path to recovery in short, frequently profound, and sometimes humorous, observations and principles about what is required to get sober, stay sober, and live life without struggle.

They have helped me, and it is my wish that they help you.

Austin, Texas —DR. RON B.
May 1993

Acknowledgments

I wish to thank the members of the Phoenix Group and the 33d Street Group and, especially, the following individuals:

John K.	Robert G.
Philip L.	Henry
Bob T.	Jack (deceased)
Dick	Bob K.
Mercedes Bob	Jack Mc.
Walt	Al
Mary	Big David
Gordon	Ted M.

1.
One day at a time.

2.
You've got to give time, time.

3.
Insanity:
Doing exactly the same thing over and over,
expecting different results.

4.
It's a good meeting if no one gets drunk
in the room during the meeting.

5.
HALT:
Hungry, Angry, Lonely, Tired.

6.
The length of time away from a drink
is not equal to the distance from a drink.

7.
You have to be able to live with yourself
before you can live with another person.

8.
It's not what happens to you
but how you perceive it.

9.
Fourth Step:
Fears, resentments, self-pities,
guilts, hatreds, and whys.

10.
This too shall pass.

11.
Happiness is an inside job.

12.
Desperation, inspiration, perspiration.

13.
Keep it simple.

14.
Turn your will and your life over to God.

15.
Don't drink even if your rear falls off;
put it in a bag and bring it to a meeting.

16.
First things first.

17.
God never closes a door
without also opening a window.

18.
Let go and let God.

19.
How important is it?

20.
Coincidence:
God performs a little
miracle and wishes
to remain anonymous.

21.
Utilize, don't analyze.

22.
An AA member is just
a drunk with a conscience.

23.
Platitudes can help your attitudes.

24.
Ninety meetings in ninety days.

25.
There's nothing wrong with pursuing happiness,
just don't get angry if it eludes you.

26.
Do the rowing and let God do the steering.

27.
Alcohol tried to murder my soul.

28.
Treat your mind like a bad neighborhood—
don't go there alone.

29.
Ten out of ten people die,
so don't take life too seriously.

30.
Only three things happen
to alcoholics who don't stop drinking:
They get screwed up, locked up, or covered up.

31.
You have to love yourself
before you can love someone else.

32.
When I have a dollar more than what I need, I'm rich.
Before I quit drinking, I was always a dollar short.

33.
You don't die when *you* get ready,
you die when God gets ready.

34.
Stand for something
or you'll fall for anything.

35.
Your actions are so loud
I can't hear what you're saying.

36.
Yesterday is so far in the past I can't see it;
tomorrow is too distant in the future to be seen.
So I'll take a good look at what I can see—today.

37.
Keep coming back.

38.
Live like this is the *last* day of your life.

39.
SLIP:
Sobriety Loses Its Priority.

40.
The best fringe benefit of being in AA
is that you never have to be alone again.

41.
Wear the world as a loose garment.

42.
Give yourself a little success every day.

43.
Only one in ten alcoholics dies sober. Beat the odds.

44.
I am responsible.

45.
But for the grace of God . . .

46.
Be profound, funny, or quiet.

47.
Trust God, clean house, and help others.

48.
God doesn't make mistakes.

49.
Any excuse for a drink
is as good as any excuse
for a drink.

50.
When tragic things begin to seem funny,
health has begun.

51.
Easy does it.

52.
After you talk in a meeting,
listen to hear if you said anything.

53.
We're all doing the best we can.

54.
Easy does it, but do it.

55.
I may have a drink tomorrow, but not today.

56.
Fake it till you make it.

57.
Put your desire chip under your tongue;
when it melts, you can have a drink.

58.
For an alcoholic, one drink
is one too many—
one thousand not enough.

59.
Never underestimate the power of prayer
or the passage of time.

60.
Meeting makers make it.

61.
No one can make you take a drink,
and no one can make you stop.

62.
Why drink today when you can
put it off until tomorrow?

63.
You have to be willing to participate
in your own recovery.

64.
A lot of people have died wanting to get sober.

65.
The great paradox of spirituality is that
you've got to give it away to keep it.

66.
This program is a marriage of hope and action,
and it has to be both.

67.
I don't need your help today.
Love,
God

68.
In the first year of sobriety,
don't change anything except your
playmates, playthings, and playgrounds.

69.
Stinkin' thinkin' leads to drinkin'.

70.
Drinkin' leads to stinkin' thinkin'.

71.
Slippery people and slippery places lead to slips.

72.
It works if you work it.

73.
Today is the yesterday
you'll worry about tomorrow.

74.
AA is a simple program for complicated people.

75.
AA is not where you wind up,
it's where you start over.

76.
Our sickness is between our ears.

77.
It takes time.

78.
You aren't going to get it by Thursday.

79.
An empty can makes the most noise.

80.
Every AA meeting is a payment
on your sobriety.

81.
Alcoholics have three choices:
die, go nuts, or get sober.

82.
God can't hand you anything new
until you let go of what you're holding.

83.
Carry your strength, hope,
and experience to those people
you find attractive and,
especially, to those you don't.

84.
When I think I'm in control,
I'm most out of control.

85.
There are many ways to cross the river—
what matters is that you cross sober.

86.
If learning to be sober doesn't feel awkward,
you're not making progress.

87.
If you don't change, you don't grow.
And if you don't grow, you don't go.

88.
Alcoholics are self-adoring egotists
who can't stand their own image.

89.
To stay sober, you must make
the abnormal normal,
and the normal abnormal.

90.
If you keep bringing your body,
your mind will follow.

91.
Alcoholism is the high cost
of low living.

92.
When confronted with a dilemma,
ask yourself,
What would God do?

93.
If you think you have humility, you don't.

94.
If others did the things to us that we
as alcoholics do to ourselves,
we'd kill them.

95.
AA is not a place to go to save your soul,
but if you have an open mind,
you may save your skin.

96.
I got drunk alone.
In AA we get sober together.

97.
In God's sight,
all human beings are important.

98.
Walk your talk.

99.
Once you give love, you receive love.

100.
You get back what you give out.

101.
You aren't responsible for anyone's
happiness but your own.

102.
You attract what you were.

103.
There are no mistakes,
just learning experiences.

104.
Want to hear God laugh?
Tell him your plans.

105.
Humility is not thinking less of yourself,
it is thinking of yourself less often.

106.
Alcoholics all drink for
the same reason—any reason.

107.
Some days are diamonds,
others just rough stones.

108.
Get out of the problem and into a solution.

109.
Live life on life's terms.

110.
Don't expect to learn about people from books;
a person can't fit in a bookcase.

111.
When I react to someone,
that person becomes my Higher Power.

112.
When you need something in your life
to replace alcohol, work a Step.

113.
My recovery is a process, not an event.

114.
HOW?
Honesty, Open-mindedness, Willingness.

115.
Do good, be good,
and God will be with you.

116.
At meetings, leave your credentials
and your intellect at the door.

117.
If you make a
Twelfth Step call
and you don't drink,
it's successful.

118.
Twelfth Step:
If they're ready, you can't say anything wrong.
If they're not, you can't say anything right.

119.
Alcohol is patient;
your disease will wait for you forever.

120.
Life is slippery when wet.

121.
Let it begin with me.

122.
We've each got our own self-improvement tool kit.

123.
Learn to listen so that you can listen to learn.

124.
You never know what
you're addicted to until you stop.

125.
It's all right to plan;
just don't plan the results.

126.
Fear is the absence of faith.

127.
The bad news:
Nobody is coming to rescue you.

The good news:
You can save yourself.

128.
I don't ever want to have to stop drinking again.

129.
I can never help another alcoholic
without helping myself.

130.
I am where I am because
that's where I'm supposed to be.

131.
The long journey to sobriety
begins where you are.

132.
Tranquilizers are nothing
more than solid alcohol.

133.
Pass it on.

134.
I have a choice.

135.
The Twelve Steps are God's gift
to the twentieth century.

136.
Before I came to AA, I never realized how
bad my life was or how good it could be.

137.
Alcohol:
Ignorant oil.

138.
I'm here because I don't
want to live like I used to live.

139.
There is little you can count on in life
except feeling bad after that first drink.

140.
Long sobriety does not mean
greater immunity from drinking again.

141.
Poor me, poor me, pour me another drink.

142.
Go to meetings when you want to,
when you need to, and at eight o'clock.

143.
Now I can wake up and say
"Good morning, God!"
rather than
"Good God, it's morning!"

144.
Many doctors believe alcoholics
suffer from a tranquilizer deficiency.

145.
AA ruined my drinking.

146.
If you don't remember your last drunk,
you haven't had it yet.

147.
When I go to extremes, I'm sure to find
misery close behind.

148.
Learn humility or you will be humiliated.

149.
People don't come into AA
because they're having a wonderful life.

150.
How has my family suffered
because I quit drinking?

151.
God gives us what we're going to need.

152.
Think! Think! Think!

153.
As long as you can stay sober,
God can talk to you.

154.
When I turned myself over to God,
I took my life out of the hands of an idiot.

155.
AA makes us into the people
we were supposed to have been.

156.
When you don't know what to do,
don't drink and go to meetings.

157.
About AA—I didn't like it,
I didn't believe it,
and it worked.

158.
Alcoholism:
Physical allergy and mental obsession.

159.
Once you have been in AA a while, you can be honest
and truthful, because you've stopped
doing things you are ashamed of.

160.
When you go to a meeting,
you're working the Twelfth Step.

161.
If I had waited to be happy until I was well,
I would still be sick.

162.
FEAR:
False Evidence Appearing Real.

163.
Things aren't any different anywhere you go.

164.
AA is a million-dollar program
purchased five cents at a time.

165.
Today I lead a life I approve of.

166.
When you're afraid,
pick up the five-hundred-pound
telephone and call someone.

167.
There is nothing wrong with your life that the removal of alcohol can't help but make better.

168.
When tempted, don't drink,
say a prayer, and go to a meeting.

169.
God, please help me.

170.
I came. I came to. I came to believe.

171.
Please God first, yourself second,
and everyone else third.

172.
It's not my luck that needs changing,
it is I.

173.
When you join AA you become a member
of the "Society of the Second Chance."

174.
When you hold on to the past with one hand
and grab at the future with the other,
you have nothing with which
you can hold on to today.

175.
You cannot get ahead until you learn to be here.

176.
If you want to get ahead with any degree of peace,
you must first learn to stay here.

177.
Even the hereafter begins with *here*.

178.
Keep an open heart.

179.
You can change only yourself,
not the rest of the world.

180.
Take a year off from worrying.

181.
I am not the center of the universe.

182.
Each day of sobriety is a testimonial
to my attempt to be a human being.

183.
When the world comes to an end, it will do
so without my permission.

184.
If I can keep my feet on the ground,
God can come down to me.

185.
To climb a ladder,
it's necessary to go up the steps.

186.
What I have to do is simple;
it's just not very easy.

187.
I thought AA would teach me how to drink,
but I already knew how to drink.
AA taught me how to live.

188.
If you don't do anything to make it better,
it will get worse.

189.
I may be mad at someone,
but I'm not going to get drunk at that person.

190.
What can I learn from this?

191.
Most of the things that irritate me
today won't be important enough
to remember tomorrow.

192.
Stop looking for the bad news
after the good news.

193.
Sometimes you just have to wait.

194.
I lived to get drunk
and got drunk to live.

195.
What can you do to take the place of drinking?
Anything in the world except drink.

196.
It hasn't been a bad day just because
a few things haven't gone my way.

197.
I only drank when I wanted to;
I just wanted to all the time.

198.
One drink: one drunk.

199.
How do you resign from AA? Take a drink.

200.
When you can't decide
if you made the right choice,
you probably didn't make either
the best or the worst choice.

201.
There are no accidents.

202.
I can't do it by myself.

203.
Come to meetings to see
those you want to be like,
as well as those you don't.

204.
If you have a slip, you lose a lot more
than just sober time.

205.
If you pray for a Cadillac
and God sends a jackass,
ride it.

206.
Think of what you have rather than what you lack.

207.
When I was drinking I had my own little world,
and it was getting smaller all the time.

208.
I have everything I need.

209.
If you still feel you have to be number one in what
you do, then be the most *human* human being.

210.
Everything you do is a step toward recovery
or toward relapse.

211.
The program of recovery is taking your old
set of values and replacing it with a new one.

212.
I'm not supposed to be drunk.

213.
I drank to kill the pain
I couldn't explain.

214.
After you get rid of alcohol,
you have to deal with the other *isms*.

215.
The worst AA meeting I ever attended
was better than my best drunk.

216.
Think about your thinking.

217.
You can lead a horse to water,
but you can't get it to buy the drinks.

218.
If you let them do it for you,
they will do it to you.

219.
Miracles can happen if no one cares
who gets the credit.

220.
How can you see life as it really is
if you view it only through the bottom of a jigger?

221.
You only have to do two things:
(1) Die, and (2) live until you die.
You make up the rest.

222.
We talked ourselves to insanity,
and we can talk ourselves back.

223.
What you think you are, you are not;
but what you think, you are.

224.
What you think about is what you become.

225.
It doesn't take much to get people on your side.

226.
God wasn't lost. I was.

227.
When I'm useful, I feel good.

228.
You can't get drunk if you
don't take that first drink.

229.
God gives us only what we can handle.

230.
I couldn't; God could.

231.
Growth: Staying green.
A plant that has no green is dead.

232.
God can't hand you a new life
until you let go of the shot glass.

233.
It's not OK for me to tell you
I'm OK when I'm not OK,
OK?

234.
Happy,
joyous, and
free.

235.
A Higher Power?
Every alcoholic had the same one:
booze.

236.
Take the program seriously, not yourself.

237.
It's OK not to be OK. People don't come
to AA because they're OK.

238.
Angry?
Remember that not everyone has a program.

239.
I'm my own problem.

240.
It's possible to be addicted to sadness.

241.
When what you're doing isn't working,
try something else—anything else, but drinking.

242.
Suicide is a permanent solution
to a temporary problem.

243.
The door to AA swings both ways.

244.
A whisky glass made a horse's ass out of me.

245.
Remember your last drunk
before you pick up your next drink.

246.
I'm only an arm's length
away from my next drink.

247.
Meetings:
The faces are different,
the problems the same.

248.
There are enough boozers out there—
they won't miss me.

249.
Alcohol was my strength;
then I learned it was my weakness.

250.
Sobriety is the greatest gift
I have ever received.

251.
I didn't grow up planning to be an alcoholic.

252.
AA is not a pretty dress you put on in the morning;
it's a way of life.

253.
There's no one too dumb for this program,
but it's possible to be too smart.

254.
You're ready for AA when
you're not drinking for fun anymore.

255.
When I was drinking, I always wanted
to be somebody else, someplace else.

256.
It's not what you want to do that matters;
it's what you do.

257.
The race is often won not by the swiftest,
but by the person who manages to keep running.

258.
It's none of my business what you think of me.

259.
Staying sober is my most important business today.

260.
Alcoholism is the only disease that
will tell you you don't have it.

261.
My alcoholism:
I was the last one to know.

262.
We plan our slips.

263.
When all else fails,
read the directions—the Twelve Steps.

264.
I have an incurable, fatal disease
which can be arrested one day at a time.

265.
I remember the lessons learned
the hard way; the easy ones I forget.

266.
All I wanted was to control you,
myself, and everything else.

267.
All is well, even when it ain't.

268.
In AA the only mistake you can make
is not coming back.

269.
My disease is an elephant.
As long as I remember it's there,
I won't get stepped on.

270.
Alcoholic:
A person with both feet planted firmly in thin air.

271.
Gratitude is the streetcar
to a better attitude.

272.
I came to AA because
I was sick and tired
of being sick and tired.

273.
Let what is given be enough.

274.
You must be, before you can do.

275.
If I don't drink today, more will be revealed.

276.
There is nothing wrong with motivation—
the key is in what motivates you.

277.
Life does not have to be a daily struggle.

278.
I accept that I cannot drink,
but that does not mean that I will not drink again.

279.
In AA you've got to surrender to win.

280.
The good is the enemy of the best.

281.
Ask God in the morning,
thank him at night.

282.
God, grant me serenity to
accept the things I cannot change . . .

283.
When I joined AA, I realized
I could run *toward* my problems.

284.
Things won't get better
because you joined AA,
but you will.

285.
Since I came to AA,
I can take a trip without taking a trip.

286.
There is dignity in sobriety.

287.
God will remove only the character defects
that stand in your way of helping others.

288.
In AA you can be a part,
not apart.

289.
Pain is inevitable,
suffering is optional.

290.
The further I'm away from my last drunk,
the closer I am to my next drink.

291.
The bad news:
When the suffering of the present
exceeds the suffering of the past,
you will drink again.

The good news:
You don't have to suffer anymore.

292.
My alcoholism is simple:
When I was drunk, I felt OK.

293.
You've got to be willing to be willing.

294.
Don't compare.

295.
You are not alone.

296.
Before you drink,
throw your desire chip in the gutter
and know that you soon will follow.

297.
I must change me,
not the geography.

298.
My problem was that if I didn't have a problem,
I would invent one.

299.
The musts, oughts, and shoulds
in your life can drive you crazy.

300.
Try praying.
Nothing pleases God more
than to hear a strange voice.

301.
How to stop drinking:
Bend your knees instead of your elbows.

302.
No matter what,
things can only get worse if you drink at them.

303.
The urge is going to pass
whether you drink or not.

304.
Before I joined AA, I was either thinking
about drinking, drinking, or getting over drinking.

305.
There was never enough
in the bottle to satisfy me.

306.
When I joined AA,
I lost my innocence about my drinking.

307.
Reality can be hell when you're only visiting.

308.
Constructive criticism:
I tell you what is wrong with you.

Destructive criticism:
You tell me what is wrong with me.

309.
God, save me from myself.

310.
Anything you would be ashamed
of doing and have not done yet,
you will do if you pick up
another drink.

311.
We're all here because we're not all here.

312.
Come to meetings to see what happens
to people who don't come to meetings.

313.
Sick, sorry, then sober.

314.
God, when I speak,
please fill my mouth with good stuff,
and give me a nudge when I've said enough.

315.
Since I joined AA, I've never needed
and wanted a drink at the same time.

316.
Plan for tomorrow, but live just for today.

317.
Please everybody and no one is pleased;
please yourself and at least you're pleased.

318.
Happiness doesn't come from getting what we want,
but from enjoying what we have.

319.
When I help, I am helped.

320.
To recover, you need something to do
and someone to love.

321.
Nothing changes until it becomes real.

322.
There is enough time to
accomplish all that is necessary.

323.
You can't expect to live a trashy
lifestyle and belong to AA.

324.
My mind is out to get me.

325.
When I joined AA,
I quit selling myself cheap.

326.
With this program I can be a decent person.

327.
The elevator of alcoholism goes only down,
but you can get off where you'd like.

328.
The longer I stay sober, the more I remember
I'd forgotten when I was drinking.

329.
Alcoholics are all from the same nut tree.

330.
Before AA I had this equation:
Self-worth = my performance + the opinions of others.
I could never get it to balance.

331.
My problems are self-made.

332.
Sober life can be distressing, but not dangerous.

333.
My worst day sober is not nearly
as bad as my worst day drinking.

334.
Alcohol endowed me with the delusion of adequacy.

335.
Alcoholic:
An egomaniac with an inferiority complex.

336.
If you hang around long enough,
someone will do the slipping for you.

337.
The load of tomorrow, added to that of yesterday,
carried today, makes the strongest falter.

338.
If I could do any better, I would.

339.
I need to get the cotton out of my ears
and put it in my mouth.

340.
I truly believed in better living through chemistry.

341.
When the student is ready, the teacher appears.

342.
As a sponsor, remember you can
carry the word, but not the person.

343.
When alcoholics are ready,
you can't keep the program from them;
when they're not, you can't give the program away.

344.
I didn't get what I wanted from AA;
I got what I needed.

345.
I never attended a meeting in which
I didn't get something, even if just angry.

346.
When I was drinking,
I was deathly afraid of living.

347.
AA works very well without me,
but I work a lot better with AA.

348.
I'm harder on myself than anybody else.

349.
It doesn't matter how you got here or
why you got here, just that you're here.

350.
People, places, and things exist
whether I choose to accept them or not.
The only choice I have about acceptance
is to be either grateful or miserable.

351.
Spiritual growth comes from being *in* AA,
not just around it.

352.
We didn't all arrive on the same ship,
but we're all in the same boat.

353.
Not drinking is easy.
It's living and not drinking that's hard.

354.
Come to ninety meetings in ninety days.
If you're not satisfied, we'll refund your misery.

355.
Two realizations have contributed
to my spiritual growth:
(1) There is a God. (2) I ain't God.

356.
All I ever wanted when I was drinking
was a little more than I ever had.

357.
Prayers don't change God,
they change me.

358.
Things I turn over to God most easily
are those things already fixed.

359.
I've failed, but I'm not a failure.
I've made mistakes, but I'm not a mistake.

360.
No one ever arrives at AA too late.

361.
You can't.
God can.
Let him.

362.
When I first got to AA, both my drinker and
my thinker were broken.

363.
Keep your mind and your body
in the same place.

364.
To get along with people,
keep skid chains on your tongue.

365.
Your greatest fear is exactly where
your alcoholism was taking you.

366.
The Serenity Prayer is the handrail to grab
until you can work the Steps.

367.
Be careful of what you do or you will
get away from what works.

368.
Alcoholics are noted for their mind-reading ability.

369.
Cease panic and start prayer.

370.
If you can't fight and you can't flee, then flow.

371.
Don't sweat the small stuff, and remember,
it's all small stuff.

372.
Drinking didn't cause my problems, living did.

373.
What comes from the heart goes to the heart.

374.
It's a lot easier to stay sober than to *get* sober.

375.
Other people's drinking never bothered
me until I quit drinking.

376.
Misery loves miserable company.

377.
There's nothing more disgusting than
being sober in a room full of drunks.

378.
It takes several years to read the black
part of the Big Book—that's the part
that's not between the lines.

379.
You don't fall off a building when
you're standing in the middle.

380.
I'm trying to be as honest as I can.

381.
AA:
Absolute Abstinence.

382.
The catch-22 of recovery:
You've got to change your thinking
to change your drinking.
But to change your thinking,
you've got to change your drinking.

383.
I began to get better when I knew I could choose
between being right and getting well.

384.
The world is not my enemy.

385.
The practicing alcoholic is the only person
in the world who can lie in the gutter and
still look down on others.

386.
If you claim to like everyone you've met in AA,
you haven't been to enough meetings.

387.
Is your mind racing?
Try reading the Big Book out loud.
Your mind can only do one thing at a time.

388.
AA meetings are the jumper cables God uses to
get love flowing from one alcoholic to another.

389.
When your time in meetings equals your
time in bars, you have a chance to recover.

390.
An alcoholic who is alone is in bad company.

391.
If it works, don't do anything to fix it.
If it doesn't work, do anything to fix it.

392.
Alcoholics don't have relationships—they take hostages.

393.
You can't be fired for on-the-job sobriety.

394.
It's a good day if I haven't harmed
myself or anyone else.

395.
I have to get out of myself to find myself.

396.
Don't pray for healing
and then tell God what to do.

397.
The only defense you have when you're wrong
is to attack.

398.
You're ready for this program when
you've drunk so much you can get neither
drunk nor sober.

399.
Don't become emotionally involved with reality.

400.
Before I came to AA, I was a human doing,
not a human being.

401.
EGO:
Easing God Out.

402.
We can't see the growth in ourselves,
but we can see it in others.

403.
By going to meetings
and working the Steps,
I may be able to make compost
out of my pile of garbage.

404.
You can't do it for anyone else.

405.
You alone can do it, but you can't do it alone.

406.
We can't take responsibility for
the sobriety of others
unless we're also willing to
take responsibility for their slips.

407.
If I'm not grateful, I'm hateful.

408.
It is not God who needs to be thanked,
but I who need to be grateful.

409.
AA is a God-centered program
for self-centered people.

410.
The most miserable person imaginable is the one
with a belly full of booze and a head full of AA.

411.
Alcoholism is not an infectious disease,
but it can be contagious.

412.
God has never been a problem in my life,
but I have been a problem to God all my life.

413.
It is more important to do what must be done
than to do all you can do.

414.
It's not so important how you started your life,
but how you finish it.

415.
When I die, I want to ride in that
long black hearse dead sober.

416.
Live and let live.

417.
When you come to AA and decide
you want what we have,
you have to do what we do.

418.
I know that I'm not yet the person I can be,
but I thank God I'm not the person I used to be.

419.
Liquor used to do things for me,
and then it began to do things to me.

420.
Practicing alcoholics are the only people
who get to choose the disease they will die from.

421.
If you're an alcoholic and you drink,
your life can only go downhill.

422.
I've never met anyone who came back after
a slip and said he or she had a good time.

423.
I drank for just two reasons:
to be what I was not and
not to be what I was.

424.
Yesterday is a canceled check,
tomorrow is a promissory note,
today is cash-on-hand.

425.
AA won't keep you from going to hell,
nor is it a ticket to heaven.
But it will keep you sober long enough
for you to decide where you want to go to.

426.
If we can only be judged by our enemies,
then, as alcoholics, we ourselves
are the best judges.

427.
Before AA I looked at the world
through dung-colored glasses.

428.
Alcoholism is the attitude disease.

429.
If you think you're happy, you are.
If you think you're wise, you are not.

430.
When I was drinking, I never
beat myself up; I always beat myself down.

431.
Alcoholic:
Someone no one likes
and who wouldn't have it any other way.

432.
It's not what you drink, nor when you drink,
nor where you drink, nor with whom you drink,
nor how often you drink;
it's *what* that *first drink* does to you.

433.
The only alcoholics who aren't guilty of driving
when drunk are those who have never driven.

434.
When I don't have expectations of others,
anything positive they do is a pleasant surprise.

435.
When I was drinking, I used to try to feel good by
buying things I didn't need, with money I didn't have,
to impress people I didn't like.

436.
I must not compare the outside of you
with the inside of me.

437.
It's my attitude toward what happens to me
that makes it a "blessin' " or a lesson.

438.
If I reached for enough drinks,
my problems wouldn't go away,
but I would.

439.
Since coming to AA, I've become inoculated
against the disease of not wanting to live.

440.
No one was ever as bad to me
as I have been to myself.

441.
Alcohol is the great solvent:
It dissolves marriages, finances,
careers, and health.

442.
AA is a fellowship of men and women who know
that other people just don't act right.

443.
AA is a fellowship of men and women who "no."

444.
The only time alcoholics will say they're
not sure is when they're positive they're right.

445.
AA will do until a cure comes along.

446.
When you come to AA, you have to learn to
be the doctor as well as the patient.

447.
You will have problems whether
or not you stay sober.

448.
I was willing to go anywhere to get a drink,
so I should be willing to go to meetings to recover.

449.
God's delay in answering our prayers
isn't God's denial.

450.
Faith is the foundation
of freedom from fear.

451.
No pain, no change.

452.
When I was drinking, there was no middle:
I believed I was absolutely perfect
or perfectly worthless.

453.
Acceptance is about what is,
not what is not.

454.
God is my friend now instead of my enemy.

455.
Tired work is never efficient.

456.
Taking that first drink is like getting hit with a freight
train—it's not the caboose that does the damage.

457.
You may not need a meeting,
but I need you to have a meeting.

458.
No matter how I lived in the past,
I can live right today.

459.
When I point my finger at you,
there are always three fingers pointing back at me.

460.
If you believe AA members gossip about you, don't worry.
AA members are so self-centered they will be back
talking about themselves very soon.

461.
God doesn't punish us for our alcoholism,
we punish ourselves with our alcoholism.

462.
SLIP:
Slight Lapse In Progress.

463.
Mean what you say, say what you mean.

464.
I didn't take a drink today, so anything is possible.

465.
The AA member with the longest sobriety
is the one who got up earliest this morning.

466.
Alcoholics are people who pole-vault over mouse turds.

467.
Loneliness is curable.

468.
I can borrow trouble only at high interest rates.

469.
Alcohol used to cause me to break out in strange spots—
London, Paris, Miami Beach.

470.
I came to AA to save my hide
and discovered my soul was attached.

471.
I worked the Steps not because I saw the light,
but because I felt the heat.

472.
If you free others to be who they are,
you'll set yourself free.

473.
Just because life has been painful so far
doesn't mean it has to keep hurting.

474.
Go for all of it and don't worry.
If you're not supposed to have it, you won't.

475.
Were we less self-centered, we'd see that
blessings and sorrows visit us all in equal amounts.

476.
Life is like the turn of a wagon wheel—
sometimes I'm in the sunshine,
and sometimes down in the mud.

477.
In the AA pasture there are lots of chips.

478.
If you pray, why worry?
If you worry *after* you pray, why pray?

479.
Having trouble turning it over to your Higher Power?
Remember that your best thinking got you drunk.

480.
If you made it this far drunk,
God won't let you down when you're sober.

481.
Hang tough!

482.
Call your sponsor before, not after,
you take that first drink.

483.
Strive to understand, rather than to be understood.

484.
To make it work,
you have to buy the whole package.

485.
The evil I dimly perceive in myself
I try to stamp out in others.

486.
Remember,
whatever position you find yourself in,
you put yourself there.

487.
We mock the things we are to be.

488.
What goes around comes around,
if you stick around.

489.
Act as if.

490.
Change is a process, not an event.

491.
Don't drink even if your rear is on fire.

492.
You can't get mugged in a dark alley
if you don't walk in dark alleys.

493.
Wherever you go, there you are.

494.
If you truly understand someone,
you will have no need to forgive that person.

495.
I'm not impatient—
I just want everything
to change right away.

496.
It took every drink I took to get here.

497.
It's amazing how this program works
when I get out of the way.

498.
Happiness is a by-product of doing the right thing.

499.
Perhaps the only purpose of my sobriety
is to stop hurting myself and others.

500.
Ego:
The sum total of false ideas about myself.

501.
Check your motives.

502.
My favorite prayer has only one word:
Help.

503.
Courage is fear that has said its prayers.

504.
My mind is not a good place to be.

505.
Do not criticize, condemn, or complain.

506.
Don't criticize others; they are just doing
what we would be doing under
similar circumstances.

507.
Why are you not happy with where you are?
Is it not exactly where you placed yourself?

508.
I'm not where I want to be,
but thank God I'm not where I was.

509.
Doing things the way I thought
they should be done is what got me here.

510.
In order to stay sober, I've got to be willing
to be part of my own life.

511.
There are no victims, just volunteers.

512.
I didn't want to stop drinking,
just to stop hurting.

513.
Sometimes it's tough to know God's will for me;
it's not posted on billboards.

514.
When I was drinking,
individual responsibility was not my strong suit.

515.
When you pray, just talk to God;
when you meditate, just listen.

516.
When I first came to the program, members said,
"Let us love you until you can love yourself."

517.
When I first came, they said, "It will get better."
I discovered the "it" was me.

518.
God is spelled G-O-D, not D-O-G,
so don't get confused and tell him to fetch.

519.
I came to AA because things began to add up,
and not add up.

520.
Meetings are really boring when I don't go.

521.
No one ever went to jail for drinking too much coffee.

522.
You get home on the ocean of your own tears.

523.
I didn't know I wanted to quit drinking
until I tried to quit drinking.

524.
I drank for just two reasons:
to feel good when I felt bad and
to feel better when I felt good.

525.
Anybody can stop drinking—just hit a cop.

526.
I didn't come to AA, because
I was afraid it would work.

Dear Reader,

If you are willing to share your favorite quote or two, you may see them in print in the next edition.

Dr. Ron B.
P.O. Box 160363
Austin, TX 78716

FAX (512) 328-3562

Rebecca Post, acquisitions editor; Caryn Pernu, manuscript editor; David Spohn, cover and interior design; Sarona Zimmerman, typesetter; Tina Petersen, copywriter; Cynthia Madsen, production editor; Joan Seim, print manager; Donald H. Freeman, managing editor; Banta Company, printer. *This book is printed in Bickley Script and Clearface.*

Notes

Notes

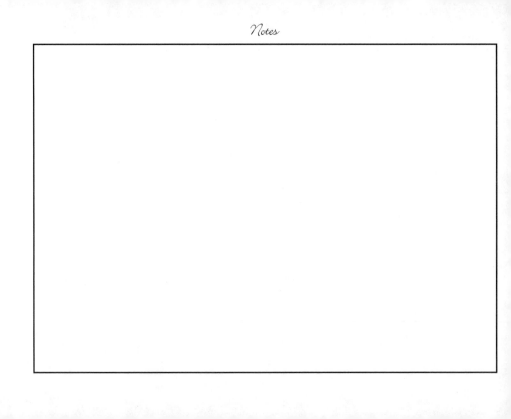

Notes

Notes

Notes

Notes

Notes